I wish you all the joy that you can wish.

— William Shakespeare

Blue Mountain Arts®

Bestselling Titles

By Susan Polis Schutz:
To My Daughter, with Love, on the Important Things in Life
To My Son with Love

By Douglas Pagels:
42 Gifts I'd Like to Give to You
100 Things to Always Remember... and One Thing to Never Forget
May You Always Have an Angel by Your Side
To the One Person I Consider to Be My Soul Mate

Is It Time to Make a Change?
by Deanna Beisser

To the Love of My Life
by Donna Fargo

Anthologies:
Always Believe in Yourself and Your Dreams
For You, My Daughter
Friends for Life
Hang In There
I Love You, Mom
I'm Glad You Are My Sister
The Joys and Challenges of Motherhood
The Language of Recovery
Marriage Is a Promise of Love
Teaching and Learning Are Lifelong Journeys
There Is Greatness Within You, My Son
Think Positive Thoughts Every Day
Thoughts to Share with a Wonderful Teenager
True Wealth
With God by Your Side ...You Never Have to Be Alone
You're Just like a Sister to Me

What I
WISH
for You

Words that would love to bring the blessings
of so many special things... to you

A Blue Mountain Arts® Collection
Edited by Douglas Pagels

Blue Mountain Press™
Boulder, Colorado

ISBN: 1-59842-056-9

Certain trademarks are used under license.
BLUE MOUNTAIN PRESS is registered in U.S. Patent and Trademark Office.

Printed in the United States of America.
First printing this edition: 2005

 This book is printed on recycled paper.

This book is printed on fine quality, laid embossed, 80 lb. paper. This paper has been specially produced to be acid free (neutral pH) and contains no groundwood or unbleached pulp. It conforms with all the requirements of the American National Standards Institute, Inc., so as to ensure that this book will last and be enjoyed by future generations.

Blue Mountain Arts, Inc.

P.O. Box 4549, Boulder, Colorado 80306

Contents
(Authors listed in order of first appearance)

You are given
a daily invitation
to fill your heart
with all the smiles
it can possibly hold.

— Douglas Pagels

Life is a great canvas; throw all the paint on
it you can.

— Danny Kaye

You have your brush, you have your colors,
you *paint paradise*, then *in* you go.

— Nikos Kazantzakis

Every day is a fresh beginning,
    Every morn is the world made new.

— Susan Coolidge

You may have a fresh start
any moment you choose.

— Mary Pickford

Life is full of new beginnings. Some change may come, something is sure to come, to close one chapter and begin another.
— Mrs. A. D. Whitney

Every man's life is a fairy-tale written by God's fingers.
— Hans Christian Andersen

My Wishes for You

May you envision today as a gift,
and tomorrow as another.
May you add a meaningful page to
the diary of each new day,
and may you make
"living happily ever after..."
something that will really come true.

And may you always keep planting
the seeds of your dreams.
Because if you keep
believing in them,
they'll keep trying their best...
to blossom for you.

— Douglas Pagels

As is the gardener, so is the garden.

— Thomas Fuller

These things I know: I have planted a garden, so I know what faith is. I have seen poplar trees swaying in the breeze, so I know what grace is. I have heard birds caroling, so I know what music is. I have seen a morning without clouds, after showers, so I know what beauty is. I have read a book beside a warm fire, so I know what contentment is. I have seen the miracle of the sunset, so I know what grandeur is.

And because I have perceived
all these things,
I know what wealth is.

— C. Weekly

Your only treasures are those which you
carry in your heart.

— Demophilus

The most important things in life
are not things.

— Anonymous

The best things are not remote and inaccessible. They are near you, within your grasp, and ever available. The best times are not in the dim future, but here and now in the living present. The best opportunities are not reserved in some distant place, but are within your reach right where you are today.

All that is good and fine and noble in life is now available to you. Resolve to claim these priceless gifts and opportunities and to use them for your largest unfoldment.

— Anonymous

All our progress is an unfolding.

— Ralph Waldo Emerson

Joys are our wings.

— Jean Paul Richter

There are joys which long to be ours.

— Henry Ward Beecher

Peace and love are always alive in us, but we are not always alive to peace and love.

— Julian of Norwich

Make peace with yourself, and heaven and earth will make peace with you.

— St. Isaak of Syria

Since life is short, we need to make it broad.
Since life is brief, we need to make it bright.

— Ella Wheeler Wilcox

You live through the darkness from what you
learned in the light.

— Hope MacDonald

There cannot be too much joy.

— Benedict de Spinoza

A Simple, Special One-Page Guide to Joy and Serenity

All our lives long, we hear the quiet advice, "Life is short. Make the most of it." And, deep in our hearts we know... that there really is a lot of wisdom behind those words.

But in the rush-a-day world we live in, where we get swamped by busy schedules and distracted by all the responsibilities placed upon us, it is so easy to forget the wisdom and the warmth of that advice.

Everyone has their ups and downs. And at times, the roller coaster ride we're on is a little scarier than we'd like it to be. But in the end, what's important is that we have a ticket to go on this journey. We are given the absolutely incredible gift of a new sunrise each and every morning. A new day! A new way of doing things. A chance to turn ordinary into extraordinary. An opportunity to get — even if it's only one little step — a little closer to our dreams, our hopes, our favorite people, and our most wonderful wishings.

And yes, maybe life is short. But when we slow down and take the time, we can't help but find... that it's very big on blessings.

— Douglas Pagels

Just to look at the sun going down behind green hills; just to watch rain falling on a quiet lake; just to see spinning tops of sand, created by winds whirling over a desert; just to be able to imagine oneself upon a ship, docking at a pier in a strange and distant port; just to be able to touch the hand of another and feel oneself become a part of that other; just to breathe the evening air and hear the voices of children, raised in laughter; O! just to feel one is a part of all the scheme of things entire — such are the blessings humans have.

— G. Allison Phelps

To be really alive means more than to be a moving, breathing, eating, drinking, and talking human creature. She who is actually alive finds the days too short for all the wonderful explorations which life offers....

She finds life itself a continual adventure, an unfolding panorama, with opportunities for pleasure and achievement at every turn.

— Ella Wheeler Wilcox

You're only here for a short visit.
Don't hurry. Don't worry. And be
sure to smell the flowers along the way.

— Walter Hagen

Hurry? I have no time to hurry.

— Igor Stravinsky

For fast-acting relief try slowing down.

— Jane Wagner

Appreciate the present hour....
Sit and hear your own breathing and look out
on the universe and be content.... One does not
have to do something to pass the time;
time can pass by itself.

— Lin Yutang

With every rising of the sun
Think of your life as just begun.

— Anonymous

Genius is childhood recaptured.

— Charles Baudelaire

How old would you be if you didn't know
how old you was?

— Satchel Paige

Whether seventy or sixteen, there is in every being's heart the love of wonder, the sweet amazement of the stars... the undaunted challenge of events, the unfailing childlike appetite for what's next, and the joy of the game of life.

— Anonymous

Will I ever be as happy again as I was when I was a child?

Maybe it would help if every now and then I let the child that shines within me live in harmony with the adult I'm required to be.

— Douglas Pagels

Look for something to be thankful and glad over each day, and you will find it.

— Ella Wheeler Wilcox

One day, with life and heart,
Is more than time enough to find a world.

— James Russell Lowell

Be a Columbus to whole new continents
and worlds within you, opening new channels,
not of trade but of thought.

— Henry David Thoreau

Think of what different worlds we discover with
a smile... rather than with a frown. Open-minded,
optimistic people just seem to color their days
in the right way, and cynics seem to do so much
to make sure their self-fulfilling prophecies come
true. Given the choice, I'll choose the same
traveling companions every time: people who set
the stage for more happiness and hope to enter
in. They're the ones who actually make those
brighter days appear... by the way they give,
by the way they live, and just by seeing things
the way they do.

— Douglas Pagels

Some people are always grumbling because roses have thorns. I am thankful that thorns have roses.

— Alphonse Karr

There is always something for which to be thankful.

— Charles Dickens

The mere sense of living is joy enough.

— Emily Dickinson

If we knew how much the habit of being thankful might do for us, I am sure we would take time out every day to count up a few of our blessings. When the spirit of thankfulness takes its place in our consciousness, we radiate life from the very center of our being to the world about us.

— Anonymous

Gratitude is heaven itself.

— William Blake

Some say a cup of camomile tea or a warm bath can induce relaxation, but gratitude is the great wooer of sleep.

— Elizabeth Yates

The world will never starve for want of wonders;
but only for want of wonder.

— G. K. Chesterton

Everything is miraculous. It is a miracle
that one does not melt in one's bath.

— Pablo Picasso

As to me I know nothing else but miracles —
To me every hour of night and day is a miracle,
Every cubic inch of space a miracle.

— Walt Whitman

Each day brings with it the miracle of a new beginning. Distractions abound, but whatever you do, don't miss the miracles.

— Douglas Pagels

Living in the past is hard work.

There can be way too much baggage to take along, and it can drag you down to the point where it's difficult to see things from the right perspective. It's better to stay light on your feet, bright in your outlook, and easy on yourself.

Living in the future?
That's no walk in the park either. Some people who live in the future spend all their time getting carried away with worry and anxiety — stressing out over the worst that could conceivably come true. They're like passengers who are so busy standing by the lifeboats that they completely miss out on the fun of the cruise.

The real gift?
It's the one we're given every day...
to open, to use any way we want,
to grow, to get better, to share with others, and to treasure so completely.

What a wonderful present it can be.

— Douglas Pagels

I got the blues
thinking of the future,
so I left off and
made some marmalade.
It's amazing how
   it cheers one up
      to shred oranges....

— D. H. Lawrence

To a young heart everything is fun.

— Charles Dickens

You deserve a life of happiness.

— Susan Polis Schutz

What sunshine is to flowers, smiles are to humanity. They are but trifles to be sure; but, scattered along life's pathway, the good they do is inconceivable.

— Joseph Addison

Have you ever noticed that the things which bring us closer to the Infinite have a laugh in them? Behold the sunshine, the birds, the flowers, the children — all laughing. Wherever you look and find goodness and beauty, you find laughter. In the dark and stormy seasons of life, our days are better lightened by kindly smiles than by sun, and better brightened by the kindly word than by the light of day.

— Anonymous

The future belongs to those who
believe in the beauty of their dreams.

— Eleanor Roosevelt

But dreams... oft are found of real events.

— Joanna Baillie

If we want to know what happiness is, we must seek it, not as if it were a pot of gold at the end of the rainbow, but among human beings who are living richly and fully the good life. If you observe a really happy man, you will find him building a boat, writing a symphony, educating his children, growing double dahlias in his garden. He will not be searching for happiness... he will have become aware that he is happy in the course of living twenty-four crowded hours in the day.

— W. Beran Wolfe

The wonder of the world,
The beauty and the power,
The shapes of things,
Their colours, lights, and shades,
These I saw.
Look ye also while life lasts.

— Words found on an old gravestone

At the close of life the question is —
Not how much you have got,
But how much you have given.
Not how much you have won,
But how much you have done.
Not how much you have saved,
But how much you have sacrificed.
Not how much you were honored,
But how much you have loved and served.

— Anonymous

Try each day to make a smile grow...
and with each low, descending sun,
there will be at least two people who
will be glad, and one of them will be you.

— John Edwin Price

Make each new morning the opening door
to a better day than the one before.

— Anonymous

I recall an account of Trollope going up to
London to pick up a rejected manuscript
from a publisher, getting on a train to
return home, laying the bulky bundle on
his lap face down, and beginning a new
book on the back pages of the rejected one.

— Anonymous

Our greatest glory is not in never falling,
but in rising every time we fall.

— Confucius

Pain is inevitable.
Suffering is optional.

— Anonymous

Life always brings new gifts to those
Whose hands are free to take them.

— Rebecca McCann

The world is a wonderful place, but it is never generous enough to blanket us with security and to let us live life with stars in our eyes.

Our optimism is always tempered with realism. And try as we might to keep them up, hopes can fade and stars can fall.

But every time I see a falling star, I'll wish for this:

That you and I will never lose the gleam that love provides to hearts that continue to hope for the best...
and very often receive it.

— Douglas Pagels

Like a morning dream, life becomes more and more bright the longer we live, and the reason of everything appears more clear. What has puzzled us before seems less mysterious, and the crooked paths look straighter — as we pass along.

— Jean Paul Richter

We must think of life as a journey.... Let us think of ways in which we can make the journey more pleasant for others as well as for ourselves. Let us remember that life's journey is good, it is thrilling, and it can be made beautiful if we do our part well.

— Seth Harmon

Today you have been given twenty-four
wonderful things: the hours in this day...
to spend in the most beautiful and
meaningful way possible.

Let this day be a reflection of
the strength that resides within you.
Of the courage that lights your path.
Of the wisdom that guides your steps.

And of the serenity that will be yours
    when this day has passed.

— Douglas Pagels

Happiness is not a station you arrive at,
    but a manner of traveling.

— Anonymous

As You Travel Through Life

I wish you a rewarding and truly remarkable journey on a trip that will take you from where you are to where you want to be.

And I hope that, each and every day, you'll get a little closer to that beautiful reality.

— Douglas Pagels

It is good to have an end to journey towards;
but it is the journey that matters, in the end.

— Ursula K. LeGuin

ACKNOWLEDGMENTS

We gratefully acknowledge the permission granted by the following authors, publishers, and authors' representatives to reprint poems or excerpts from their publications.

The Zondervan Corporation for "You live through the darkness..." from WHEN ANGELS APPEAR by Hope MacDonald. Copyright © 1982 by Hope MacDonald. All rights reserved.

HarperCollins Publishers for "For fast-acting relief..." from THE SEARCH FOR SIGNS OF INTELLIGENT LIFE IN THE UNIVERSE by Jane Wagner. Copyright © 1986 by Jane Wagner, Inc. All rights reserved.

The New York Times for "You're only here for..." by Walter Hagen, from THE NEW YORK TIMES, May 22, 1977. And for "How old would you be..." by Satchel Paige, from THE NEW YORK TIMES, June 8, 1984. Copyright © by The New York Times. All rights reserved.

Walker and Company, a division of the Walker Publishing Company, Inc., for "It is good to have..." from THE LEFT HAND OF DARKNESS by Ursula K. LeGuin. Copyright © 1969 by Ursula K. LeGuin. All rights reserved.

A careful effort has been made to trace the ownership of selections used in this anthology in order to obtain permission to reprint copyrighted materials and give proper credit to the copyright owners. If any error or omission has occurred, it is completely inadvertent, and we would like to make corrections in future editions provided that written notification is made to the publisher:

BLUE MOUNTAIN ARTS, INC., P.O. Box 4549, Boulder, Colorado 80306

L